W9-AWJ-428

superstars! superstars! superstars superstars

CREATIVE EDUCATION SPORTS SUPERSTARS

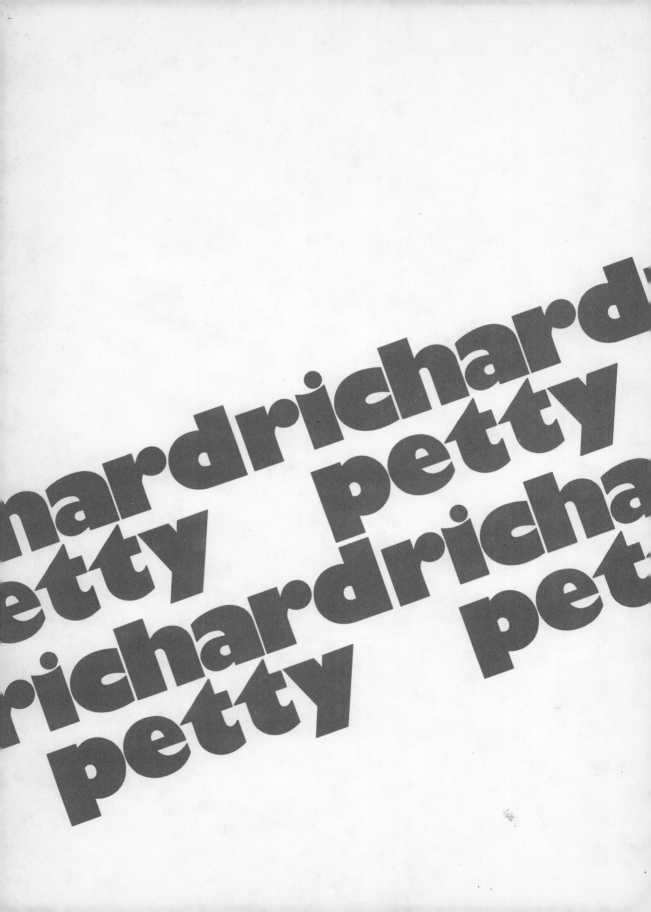

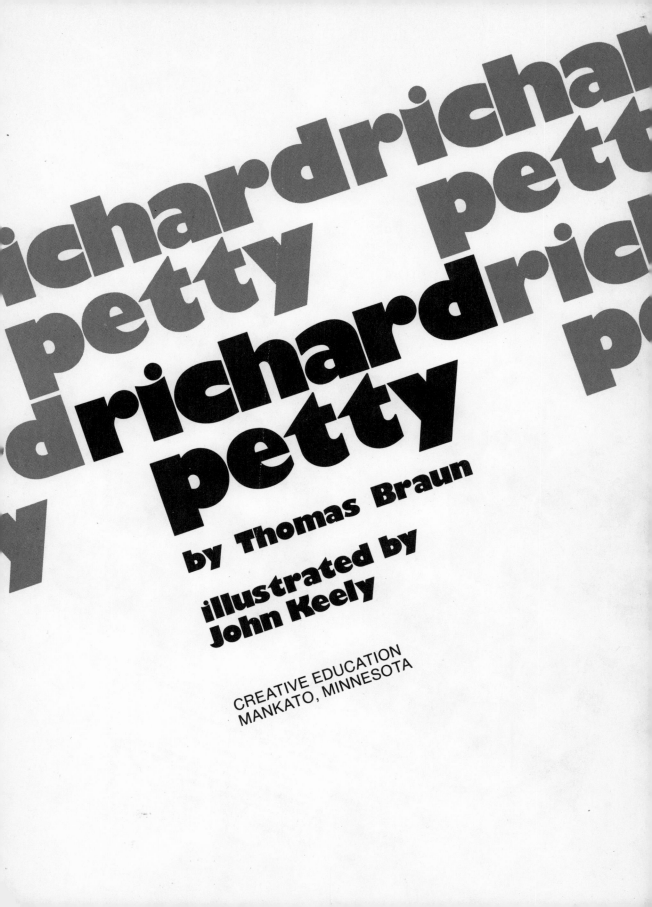

richard petty

by Thomas Braun

illustrated by
John Keely

CREATIVE EDUCATION
MANKATO, MINNESOTA

nardrichard
etty petty
richardricha
petty pet

Published by Creative Educational Society, Inc., 123 South Broad Street, Mankato, Minnesota 56001.
Copyright © 1976 by Creative Educational Society, Inc. International copyrights reserved in all countries.
No part of this book may be reproduced in any form without written permission from the publisher.
Printed in the United States.
Distributed by Childrens Press, 1224 West Van Buren Street, Chicago, Illinois 60607.
Library of Congress Number: 75-37887 ISBN: 0-87191-500-6
Library of Congress Cataloging in Publication Data
Braun, Thomas, 1944- Richard Petty.
SUMMARY: A brief biography of the stock car driver considered to be the best in the world.
1. Petty, Richard–Juvenile literature. 2. Automobile racing–Juvenile literature.
(1. Petty, Richard. 2. Automobile racing–Biography)
I. Keely, John. II. Title.
GV1032.P47B72 796.7'2'0924 (B) (92) 75-37887 ISBN: 0-87191-500-6

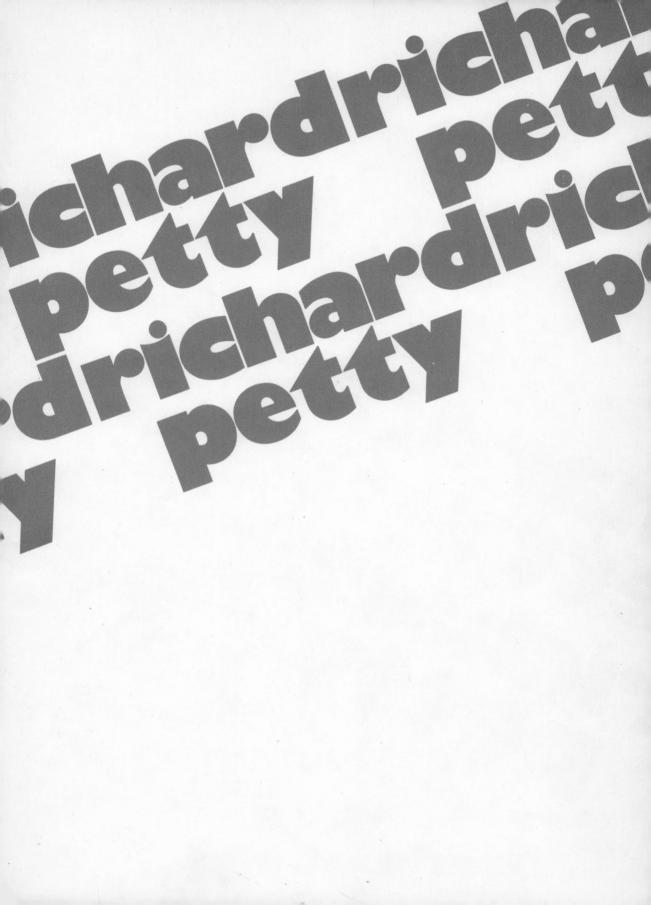

From a distance Richard Petty looks and talks like a simple country boy. He's tall, strong and friendly. His grin is wide and easy. He drinks Pepsi, eats popcorn and still calls his father "Daddy." But get closer and look harder: Richard Petty drives stock cars on NASCAR's Grand National circuit. Richard finds the groove up high on the super-ovals. With fast pitting and careful drafting, he often slingshots past the leader at the finish to take the checkered flag.

From a distance the sport of auto racing looks simple too—put a driver in a car and see how fast he can go. But get closer and look harder and suddenly auto racing—like Richard Petty—looks more complicated than the inside of a double-barreled carburetor. The organizations, classifications, equipment and technology make the sport as mysterious as an imaginary game that combines the rules of football, hockey and, maybe, Monopoly.

Different classes of cars run on different shaped tracks in races sanctioned by different national organizations. There are stock cars, sport cars, formula cars and dragsters. They run on oval tracks, drag strips or road courses. Races

are governed by such groups as USAC, NASCAR, SCCA, and NHRA.

Judged by the number of races run in each category and the number of fans attending each race, clearly the most popular class of professional auto racing is stock car racing. Located between Brookings, South Dakota and Daytona Beach, Florida, there are more than 2000 stock car tracks in the United States. Excluding horse racing, more people attend stock car competitions than attend any other professional spectator sport and that includes baseball and football.

The National Association for Stock Car Auto Racing or NASCAR for short, supervises four divisions of stock car competition: Hobby, Sportsman, Modified Sportsman and Grand National. The division with the biggest tracks, the fastest cars and the most prize money—the division long dominated by Richard Petty—is the Grand National circuit.

Since his first race in 1958, Richard Petty has become the best stock car driver in the world. The claim can be supported easily by his amazing record.

By the end of the 1974 racing season, Richard had won 164 Grand National races, more than any other driver. His closest competitor was David Pearson with a career total of 84 wins. Richard has won the Daytona 500, NASCAR's best known race, 5 times. No other driver has won at Daytona more than once. In 1971, he became the first stock car driver to win more than a million dollars during a career. His earnings for the 1971 season alone were $309,225, another record. In 1975 he is expected to pass the $2 million mark.

A stock car race is more than just a race. It's a total event with sounds and smells and excitement that defy second-hand description. As any real race fan knows, "Ya gotta be there."

Every fall in Darlington, South Carolina, popping beer cans compete with popping Confederate rifles. On Labor Day a small band of Confederate soldiers fights a predictable battle against a squad of blue-coated Yankees. As the cannons stop barking and the smoke clears, the Union troops always surrender. The rebels cheer their rigged victory, then pack away their gray uniforms for another year.

This mock-Civil War battle is only one part of the week-long celebration which precedes the oldest and most important 500-mile race in NASCAR competition—the Southern 500.

The annual celebration at Darlington opens with a golf tournament on the weekend before the race. During the week, thousands of race fans arrive in cars, pick-up trucks, vans, campers, minibikes and motorcycles. The busiest newcomers are the stock car drivers and their crews, who compete in time trials on Wednesday, Thursday and Friday. The fastest forty-four cars qualify for Monday's race. On Saturday, a parade and a beauty pageant follow a consolation race among cars which have not qualified. Sunday night everyone attends a huge party in the oval infield of the Darlington International Raceway. Big people and little people dressed in swim suits, T-shirts and tied-up blouses keep trying one last piece of fried chicken.

In the hot, late days of August, 1966, Richard Petty crosses the border between North and South Carolina and continues south through Cheraw and Dovesville toward Darlington. He is driving a trailer truck. Inside, protected by a form-fitting canvas cover, is a blue Plymouth. This is no ordinary blue Plymouth. It is a hand-tooled machine which has been assembled and checked-out with as much care as a lunar landing module. Richard has unloaded his cars at the Darlington garage area before. But in six record-breaking years on the Grand National circuit, he has never won the Southern 500. For Richard and his crew, that fact makes going to work this time more important than usual.

On the first day of qualifying laps, Richard arrives at the track early. He has left his wife and three children at a nearby motel. Before he can take some practice laps on the track, his Plymouth, like all the other stock cars entered in the contest, must undergo close inspection. NASCAR provides sharp-eyed technical inspectors who carefully examine the cars. More than 100 checks must be made to assure both safety and conformity to NASCAR regulations. The engine cylinders are measured. The inspector checks the length of the wheelbase, the size of the gas tank and the overall weight of the car. All safety devices, such as the firewall separating the engine from the driver, must be in perfect order.

The NASCAR inspector informs Richard's crew that

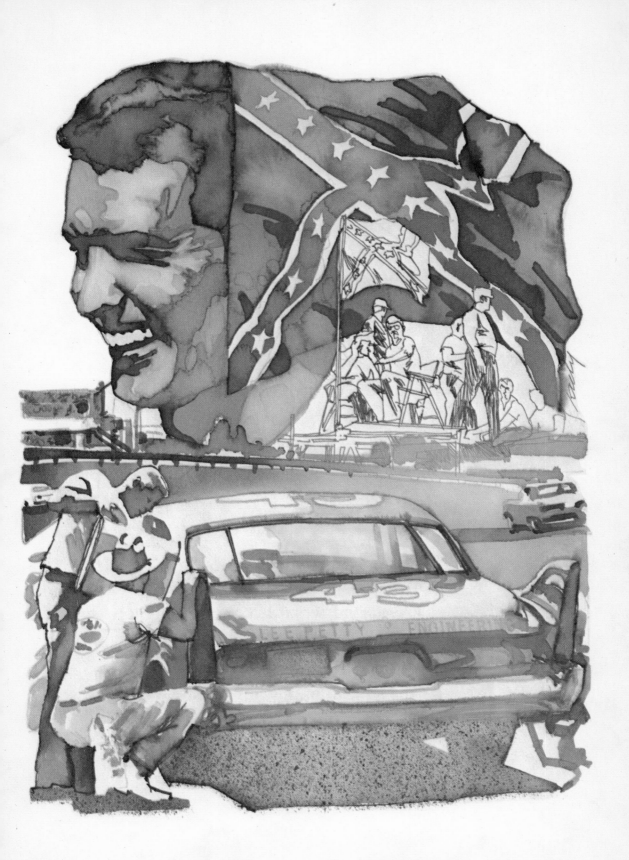

their Plymouth is 25 pounds below the 3,800-pound minimum weight. Someone bolts an extra 25 pounds of metal into the car's trunk. Richard is in a huddle with the three most important members of his crew—his father, Lee; his brother, Maurice; and a cousin, Dale Inman. They examine a small black notebook. After every race Dale and Maurice record critical information about their car's performance. They note which tires work best. Having run numerous races at Darlington, they have recorded every possible detail about the track itself. It's a tough track. More than one driver has said that driving 500 miles at Darlington is as difficult as driving 1000 miles on any other oval.

Darlington, like all race tracks, has its own "groove"; and, to win, Richard knows he must find the groove and stay in it. The groove on any track is the particular line or path that a car takes around a track in order to achieve the highest possible speed. Usually a driver will approach a tight turn on the outside of the track; then as he nears the center of the turn, he drops down to the inside. Leaving the turn he swings outside again. This path or groove marks the quickest way through the turn without throwing the car into a dangerous skid. In the early days of racing on dirt tracks, car after car would follow this same line through a turn and an actual rut or groove would be worn in the dirt. On the newer asphalt tracks the groove is often indicated by a thin black line of tire-rubber etched on the track by the cars.

One lap around the Darlington track consists of a straightaway, two steep, highly-banked turns, another straightaway and then much flatter third and fourth turns.

Richard is aware of another, more famous characteristic of this 1⅜-mile oval. The groove in the third turn is so close to the white metal guard rail on the outside that a fast car will often scrape the rail just slightly. Anything more than a soft scrape and the car will be thrown into a spin. The maneuver leaves a thin, white line on the car's right rear bumper. The drivers refer to this white badge of courage as the "Darlington Stripe."

Richard takes a few practice laps, then returns to the pit area in the infield and watches the other drivers take their laps. He says he can learn more about track conditions and how his car will handle by watching other drivers than by actually taking the laps himself. He checks the temperature, the humidity, and the wind velocity, then takes another look at his tires.

On the first day of qualifying for the Southern 500, no less than eight drivers break the track record. Richard easily qualifies by pushing his Plymouth to 139.701 miles per hour. But there is someone else driving even faster. Lee Roy Yarbrough surprises everyone by hitting 140.058 m.p.h. and winning the "pole position." Lee Roy will start the race on the inside in the first row of cars. Richard will be next to him in the first row on the outside. The rest of the starting order is determined by Friday night. Then the drivers anxiously wait out the week-end festivities.

Early Monday morning rain showers fall briefly. Close to 70,000 people begin filling the grandstand. Some fans find seats on temporary scaffolds set up on tops of cars and trucks in the infield. The rain has increased the humidity. It's going to be hot. As crew members haul big red cans of gasoline into the pits, a parade of famous old stock cars and less-famous new beauty queens circles the track. A helicopter suddenly appears over the infield. It drops down gently

and unloads a preacher who walks to a microphone and leads the drivers and fans in a short prayer. The sound of the prayer is replaced by the nervous whine of airwrenches being checked in the pits. For rapid tire changes during the race, the wrenches, powered by compressed air, must function perfectly.

At 11 A.M. the track announcer says, "Gentlemen start your engines." Richard Petty climbs through the open window on the driver's side of his number 43 Plymouth. The doors are welded shut on all stock cars to protect the drivers. He fastens a rope safety net over the window and starts the engine. The drivers quickly find their starting positions. Twenty-two pairs of glistening cars follow politely behind the pace car. Looking like twin roller-coasters nearing the top of a steep climb, the two tight lines glide slowly through the first and second turns, then through the far straightaway. Out of the fourth turn, the pace car abruptly becomes a frightened white rabbit and darts to safety into the pit lane. The starter waves his flag and the announcer's familiar shout, "AND THEY'RE OFF" gets lost in the thunder of exploding engines.

The only people seated are the drivers. The spectators all stand and cheer the rolling start of the 364-lap contest. Paul Goldsmith in a Plymouth immediately breaks out of his second row position and takes the lead. Richard and Lee Roy Yarbrough drop in behind him. On the sixth lap Richard jumps into the lead. But only one lap later, both Yarbrough and a newcomer, Darel Dieringer, spurt out in front of Richard. Yarbrough's Dodge Charger holds onto the lead for the next 24 laps. Richard lets two more cars break in front of him and drops back to fifth position. The lead keeps changing. A Comet passes a Ford, then another Ford passes the Comet.

Near the end of the first 100 laps, blue number 43 becomes the first car to regain the lead. But by lap 188, the lead has changed ten more times. On lap 189 a Dodge blows a tire in the first turn, smacks the right side of Richard's Plymouth, bounces high up into the outside guard rail, then swerves back down into the infield. The crash temporarily brings out the yellow caution flag. Under a yellow flag, cars must maintain their order. No one can pass. Because of this rule, it's a good time for a pit stop.

Richard's car is not damaged; but the heat is beginning to blister his tires and he needs fuel. He heads for the

pit. A pit stop or "pitting" is a kind of high-speed mini-ballet during which five crewmen change tires, fill the gas tank, clean the windshield and give the driver water and as much encouragement as time allows.

As Richard pulls into his own pit area, Maurice jumps the low guard rail yelling, "Get me a tire up here." The 180° asphalt has done its customary damage to the rightside tires. Maurice and Dale jack up the car and start replacing both right tires; someone else feeds the car ten gallons of gas, Lee Petty feeds his son some water and clears away dust and bits of rubber from the windshield, the air wrenches spin five lug nuts on the new wheels, the jack is pulled out, and, after 19.5 seconds, less time than it takes to read this sentence, Richard guns his Plymouth back onto the track.

After 200 laps most of the cars are forced to drop back, unable to maintain the pace set by the remaining leaders. Dieringer takes and holds the first position until Richard takes it away again on lap 246. Dieringer moves his Comet within inches of Richard's back bumper and stays there. The Comet is "drafting" the Plymouth.

Drafting is an arrangement which allows two cars to go faster together than either can can go separately. Moving at top speed, a single car pushes through the air just as a boat pushes through water. The single car is slowed both by wind resistance from the front and a kind of pulling or vacuum effect from the back. When two cars run bumper-to-bumper, the front car has front resistance but no drag resistance and the second car has drag resistance but no front resistance. By drafting, total resistance on two cars is reduced and the two cooperating cars can increase their speed. There is, however, one disadvantage to the drafting arrangement for the front runner. At the right moment, the second car can turn out and experience a "slingshot" effect which actually throws him ahead of the front car.

Dieringer, however, is unable to slingshot past Richard. On lap 330 Dieringer's crew signals a fuel stop. The Comet swings into the pit area, Richard increases his lead and, with only eight laps remaining, seems to be the sure winner.

Suddenly, the spectators see Richard making an un-expected turn into the pit lane. The Plymouth is running out of gas. By the time the car is refueled, the Comet is leading by a lap. Richard pushes to catch up. In the critical third turn he slams the guard rail too hard. He has picked up the Dar-lington Stripe—and more. His right front tire is flat. A flat tire with just over one lap to go. Richard Petty is able to limp the final lap on the inner safety tire but he crosses the finish line 41 seconds behind the winner of the 1966 Southern 500, Darel Dieringer.

Losing at Darlington was a bitter disappointment for Richard. In 1959, 1960, 1963, 1964 and then again in 1966, he had come close to winning the Southern 500. But each time another car had squeezed by number 43 in the last few laps. Richard wasted no time looking back. The National 500 at Charlotte was not far off. After that would come the American 500, The Daytona 500, the World 600 and the Firecracker 400. There would be still other big races and numerous shorter ones during the long stock car season. His reputation as the top NASCAR driver had not been made by fretting over losses. Richard had grown up and matured in a racing world where the only thing worth worrying about was winning.

About 30 miles south of Greensboro, North Carolina, is the small town of Randleman. A few miles outside of Randleman is the tiny town of Level Cross. In a white house at the end of a dirt road outside of Level Cross is where Richard Petty was born. Long before Richard's birth on July 2, 1938, Lee Petty had begun shaping his son's future. When he was 16 years old, Lee traded a bicycle for an old Model T Ford. Since that moment automobiles have dominated the lives of the entire Petty family.

Lee has always loved cars. He ran a small trucking business but spent every free minute repairing and rebuilding secondhand cars. Soon he was discovering how to make factory-built engines more powerful. Often at night on the dark North Carolina highways, Lee and his neighbors raced against each other.

At about the same time, Richard and his friends started racing too. Their competition was confined first to toy cars, then to wagons. Richard remembers greasing the wheels of his red wagon and adding weights to make it move faster down the hill. Richard outgrew wagon races quickly and turned to racing bicycles. The boys laid out a narrow, hilly course through the woods. They added a deep water hole at the bottom of one of the hills and ended up with the most treacherous bike track in North Carolina. Luckily, another nearby swimming hole offered a place to clean both bikes and riders before heading home for dinner.

Richard's boyhood races just shortly preceded the national organization of professional stock car racing in 1948. In that year a former filling station attendant named Bill France met with a small group of stock car jockeys and formed the association called NASCAR. Since that meeting, NASCAR has written and enforced the rules which govern all stock car contests. A second important event in stock car history occurred in 1949 when the first super-speedway was constructed at Darlington. Races were still being held on flat, dirt tracks; but at Darlington, with its steeply banked turns and long stretches of hard asphalt, drivers could run faster and longer than on any other track in the country.

As stock car competition was gaining the recognition and respect brought on by better organization and improved tracks, Lee Petty was becoming a famous driver. In 1954, 1958 and 1959, he won the Grand National Championship, a title determined by total points won during a full season. Until 1967 he held the record for the most career victories.

During the years that Lee Petty dominated the race scene, Richard and his brother Maurice were turning into expert auto mechanics. They both gained valuable experience building cars and working on their father's pit crew.

In one of Richard's first days in the pits, he made an unforgettable error. Lee pulled in for a tire change and Richard noticed his father's windshield was caked with mud. He jumped on the hood to scrape off the dirt. Lee shot back onto the track and discovered half-way through the lap that his wide-eyed son was stretched flat out, clinging desperately to the hood. Lee had to make an unscheduled pit stop. With a sharp glare, Lee deposited his startled passenger back in the pits and re-entered the race. Richard had, rather unconventionally, completed his first lap of NASCAR competition.

At Randleman High School, Richard was a good student and an excellent athlete. But like his father, he was always preoccupied with cars. Soon after his 21st birthday, he approached his father and stated with some caution, "I think I'm ready to drive."

Without hesitating, Lee pointed to an old Oldsmobile

behind the house, "OK, you can fix-up that one over there."

Richard worked for days, tuning the old car. He painted a big "43" on the side (Lee's number was 42); and before the paint was dry, he and his cousin, Dale, towed the Oldsmobile to a 100-mile race in Columbia, South Carolina. As the green flag waved the start, Richard grabbed the wheel and took off. His spectacular NASCAR career started that day with a very unspectacular sixth-place finish.

At the end of his first season, Richard had won a total of 76 dollars and wrecked several of his father's cars. Nevertheless, both father and son felt confident that Richard had the skill and temperament to become a great driver.

The next year Richard didn't win any of the 8 races he entered, but 5 times he managed to finish among the top 5 drivers. His season earnings topped $10,000 and the members of NASCAR voted him Rookie of the Year. All of these accomplishments were important, but the highlight of that second season was his marriage to Lynda. A former cheerleader at Randleman High School, Lynda now led cheers for the Petty team.

Richard's skill as a driver rapidly increased. In February, 1960, he won his first NASCAR race on the

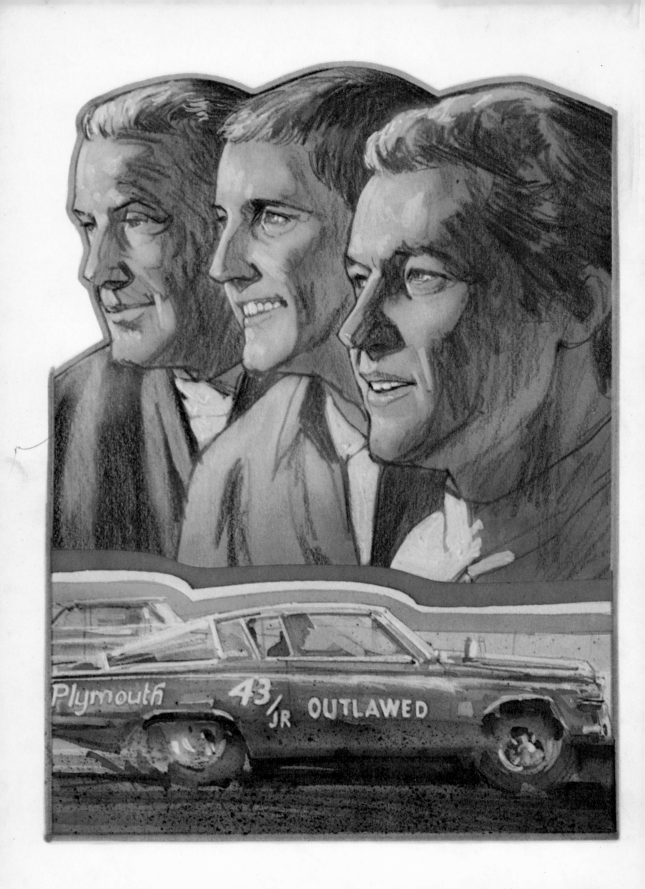

half-mile dirt track at Charlotte. Every year between 1961 and 1964 he was voted "Most Popular Driver." In 1964 he won the Daytona 500 and the Grand National Championship both for the first time.

Before the start of the 1965 season, NASCAR officials outlawed the powerful "hemi-engine" designed by Chrysler and used in Petty Plymouths. In protest, Richard dropped out of stock car racing and spent most of the season competing on drag strips.

Richard's career as a drag racer was brief and tragic. One afternoon in Dallas, Georgia, something snapped in his car's left front suspension. Unable to steer or brake, Richard's car skidded up an embankment, jumped high in the air and smashed down into a crowd of spectators. Richard was thrown clear. Six people were seriously injured. An 8-year old boy died.

Richard has been involved in several serious wrecks,

and his father was forced into retirement after being nearly crushed to death in a race at Daytona. But that sad afternoon in Georgia was the darkest day of Richard's career.

At the end of the 1965 season, the Petty team returned to stock car racing. In 15 starts, Richard won four minor races. He won more contests in 1966, including another Daytona 500 victory, and narrowly lost the Southern 500 to the rookie, Dieringer.

The absence of a victory at the big Darlington Labor Day race didn't last long. In late August, 1967, Richard again drove his trailer truck into South Carolina. This time he had 21 season victories behind him. He had broken Lee's record for career wins in May, and he had set a new record for season wins in mid-August.

Before the race, the same Confederate soldiers fought the same Civil War battle. More fans ate more fried chicken. After the new queens waved to the crowd and the preacher announced his prayer, Richard fired up his 404-cubic-inch engine and drove one of the best races of his life. He picked up the "Darlington Stripe" early. At the three-quarter mark he was two laps ahead of the rest of the field. That lead increased to 3 laps, then to 4. Bumper stickers throughout the raceway proclaimed "Richard Petty for President," but no driver got close enough to "draft" Richard. He crossed the finish line 5 full laps ahead of the second place car. He had led the race for 345 of the 364 total laps. Only three other cars had briefly led the race. In victory-lane Richard got his first Southern 500 trophy and a kiss from Lynda.

Since the big win at Darlington in 1967, the Petty team has been winning races with almost tedious regularity. A recent newspaper carried banner headlines about all the glory and money won by Bobby Unser at the Indy 500. Hidden on the last page of the sports section in an article smaller than some want-ads was news that Richard had set a new speed record and won the World 600 at Charlotte, North Carolina. The sports editor should have been more impressed. The Charlotte Speedway was the only major track in the country on which Richard had not previously won a race. There are few records left to break.

Ask him about his records, his money, and his fame as a racing legend, and Richard Petty will probably grin, throw his long arm around his 15-year old son, Kyle, and say, "We're just simple country folk, really."

JOHN HAVLICEK
JULIUS ERVING
JACKIE ROBINSON
MUHAMMAD ALI
O. J. SIMPSON
JOHNNY BENCH
WILT CHAMBERLAIN
ARNOLD PALMER
A. J. FOYT
JOHNNY UNITAS
GORDIE HOWE
WALT FRAZIER
PHIL AND TONY ESPOSITO
BOB GRIESE

LAURA BAUGH
PELÉ
JACK NICKLAUS
BILL RUSSELL
MARK SPITZ
VINCE LOMBARDI
BILLIE JEAN KING
ROBERTO CLEMENTE
JOE NAMATH
BOBBY HULL
HANK AARON
JERRY WEST
TOM SEAVER

superstars! superstars! superstars!

CREATIVE EDUCATION SPORTS SUPERSTARS

FRANK ROBINSON
PANCHO GONZALES
LEE TREVINO
KAREEM ABDUL JABBAR
JEAN CLAUDE KILLY
EVONNE GOOLAGONG
ARTHUR ASHE
SECRETARIAT
ROGER STAUBACH
FRAN TARKENTON
BOBBY ORR
LARRY CSONKA
JOHNNY MILLER
FRANCO HARRIS
BOB McADOO

BILL WALTON
ALAN PAGE
PEGGY FLEMING
OLGA KORBUT
DON SCHULA
MICKEY MANTLE
EVEL KNIEVEL
JIMMY CONNORS
CHRIS EVERT
PETER REVSON
KATHY WHITWORTH
JACKIE STEWART
STAN SMITH
JANET LYNN
RICHARD PETTY